THE FOUR NOAHS

IF IT'S MEANT TO BE,
IT'S UP TO ME

Other books by Brian A. Peters :

The METUS Principle:
Recognizing, Understanding and Managing Fear

Not So Common Sense:
Threats and 21st Century American Democracy

The Pocket Guide to Leadership:
The 9 Essential Characteristics for Building
High-Performing Organizations

THE FOUR NOAHS

IF IT'S MEANT TO BE, IT'S UP TO ME

BRIAN A. PETERS

MAVENMARK BOOKS
MILWAUKEE, WISCONSIN

Published by
MavenMark Books, an imprint of
HenschelHAUS Publishing, Inc.
www.henschelHAUSbooks.com

Paperback ISBN: 978159598-421-0
Hardcover ISBN: 978159598-422-7
E-ISBN: 978159598-423-4
LCCN: 2015912902

Publisher's Cataloging-In-Publication Data
(Prepared by The Donohue Group, Inc.)

Names: Peters, Brian A. | Cash, Melisa, illustrator.
Title: Four Noahs : if it's meant to be, it's up to me / Brian A. Peters ; illustrations by
    Melisa Cash.
Other Titles: If it's meant to be, it's up to me
Description: Milwaukee, Wisconsin : MavenMark Books, an imprint of HenschelHAUS
    Publishing, Inc., [2016]
Identifiers: LCCN 2015912902 | ISBN 978-1-59598-421-0 (paperback) | ISBN 978-1-
    59598-422-7 (hardcover) | ISBN 978-1-59598-423-4 (ebook)
Subjects: LCSH: Attitude (Psychology) | Motivation (Psychology) | Noah's ark. | Bible--
    Parables. | Success.
Classification: LCC BF327 .P48 2016 (print) | LCC BF327 (ebook) | DDC 152.4--dc23

Cover design and illustrations by Melisa Cash

Printed in the United States of America

To my daughters,
Kensington & McKinley.

Always remember to work hard,
give your best effort,
and have faith.

With love,
Dad

TABLE OF CONTENTS

ACKNOWLEDGMENTS

Thank you to the following people, who so generously gave of their time and energy to provide feedback and recommendations on *The Four Noahs*: Dr. Steve Bialek, Heidi Goelzer, Michael Hosford, Sharon Lechter, Chris Kapenga, Connie Pasierb, and Scott Schultz.

In addition, I would like to thank Melisa Cash for her creative illustrations and cover design.

PREFACE

If you are reading this book, there's a chance you also read the book *Who Moved My Cheese?* by Dr. Spencer Johnson.

Dr. Johnson did a magnificent job using a simple story that offered a strong message in a very succinct and memorable way.

Much like with Hollywood movies, our favorite must-see TV sitcoms, reality TV shows, and count-less novels, I thought it advantageous to use Johnson's narrative template to communicate my own message and advice. A frequent question in society is, "Why reinvent the wheel?" Other advice is "Keep it simple." And so I present my own simple wheel—and like that of *Who Moved My Cheese?*—I hope it travels well.

INTRODUCTION

WHETHER YOU ARE FROM THE UNITED States, North America, the Western Hemisphere, or simply reside somewhere on the planet Earth, it is likely that you have heard the story of an epic flood of historic proportion. The story of this Great Flood exists in ancient texts and oral tradition that span cultures, religions and nations.

For those not familiar with the story of the Great Flood, those who could use a brief refresher, those of you who like a good story, and even those of you who know the story well—allow me to do my best to provide you with a brief introduction...

THE MAN AND HIS MESSAGE

ONE DAY, A MAN ENCOUNTERED A VISITOR, who claimed to have a message of great significance. Intrigued by the Visitor, the man listened intently.

"I want you to build a boat, but not just any boat. This boat, which shall be called an ark, will be a massive structure 450 feet long, 50 feet wide and 30 feet tall. It must be made of the finest wood you can find, cut with precision and constructed to my exact specifications."

The Visitor continued, "Once you have finished building the ark, you are to go out in search of all of creatures on Earth, and bring aboard two of each, one male and one female. Also, make sure you bring aboard enough food for your family and the animals to last at least one year."

In a deep voice, the Visitor went on. "There will be a Great Flood. It will rain for 40 days and 40 nights, and water will cover the planet in its entirety for 150 days. More than one year will pass before it will then be safe to step foot off the ark.

"If you listen to my words—and only if you follow my directions with precision and care—you, your family, and all the creatures aboard the ark will be safe. When a total of 430 days have passed, I will meet you and assist you back onto land."

As the man listened to the Visitor, it was as if the message was recording in his head, for he was able to recall every detail with crystal clarity.

However, he had one question: "How much time do I have to complete such a monumental task?

The Visitor replied, "You have 120 years, my friend. Make the best of them."

With those words, the Visitor was gone. His departure happened as quickly and inconspicuously as he had appeared.

You might recognize this man to be Noah. But what if I told you that this Noah wasn't the only person to receive this message? What if there were other Noahs? Continue reading the story of *The Four Noahs*.

FOUR NOAHS: THE STORY

LONG AGO, IN A LAND QUITE SIMILAR to our own, lived four men.

Each of these four men was quite different, but they did possess two things in common: their name and their ability to hear and recall information with complete clarity.

Each of the men was named Noah, and by virtue of that name, and that name alone, each was paid a visit from a wise, but mysterious, stranger.

Seemingly out of nowhere, this Visitor appeared, claiming to have a message of great significance. As the Visitor began to speak, each of the four Noahs reacted in a similar manner—that is, each looked around to see who else was in their presence.

In every instance, Noah realized he was alone.

None of the Noahs wanted to pass up a good conversation, so each reacted much the same way—he listened. Carefully, each Noah noted every word the Visitor offered, making certain not to miss a single one.

Despite there being four separate encounters, thousands of miles from one another, the message was both spoken and heard in exactly the same way. There was not a single difference in the conversations from one Noah to the next.

Each Noah was told that he had been chosen for a great and noble purpose, and with that purpose, came great responsibility.

"Noah," the Visitor said to each man, "you are special. You have been chosen to carry out a very important, very difficult, and very lengthy project. It is a project that not only affects your life, but those of many others around you. This project will also impact every human being and living creature for centuries to come."

Given the magnitude of the stranger's statement, each Noah reacted much the same way, thinking to himself, "Why me? I am no one special. I am simply one of thousands just like me. I possess no special skills or talents that are undeniably unique. For what reason has this stranger come to visit me?"

Nonetheless, each Noah continued to listen.

The Visitor went on. "Noah, I need you to build a boat, but not just any boat. It will be called an ark that will serve as your home for more than one year—not only for you, but also for your family, along with two of every animal that can be found— one male and one female of each.

For a moment, each Noah wondered if his ears were deceiving him. Was this stranger truly asking him to build a floating home capable of housing his family, along with hundreds, if not thousands, of animals?

The Visitor explained, "Noah, a great flood is coming. A flood unlike any you have ever seen or ever imagined. It will rain for 40 days and 40 nights. It will rain so relentlessly that every piece of land you have ever known will be immersed in water. After the rains stop, the entire earth will remain covered with water for nearly half a year. It will not be safe for you to set foot upon land for 8 months beyond that."

The feeling, oh, the overwhelming feeling. "Why me?" thought each Noah.

But the Visitor wasn't finished.

"To shelter both your family and the creatures, you will need to construct a vessel that is 450 long, 50 feet wide, and 30 feet tall, with an entrance on the side to bring them aboard. It must be made of the finest wood you can find, cut with precision to exact my specifications."

The Visitor continued. "Look around, Noah. We are alone. If you cut corners, only you will know it."

With the pressure mounting, each Noah began to look increasingly concerned. The Visitor smiled at each Noah in return.

"Now, I suppose you are waiting for the best part?" the Visitor asked each Noah.

"Is there a best part?" each Noah asked hesitantly.

"Of course there is, my boy!" replied the Visitor, with excitement in his voice. "You didn't think I would come all this way, and go through all this effort, unless there was a best part, did you?"

Each Noah stared at the Visitor for a moment before finally inquiring, "Then what is it?"

"I'm glad you asked," said the Visitor. "The best part is that if you listen to my advice, trust what I have told you, and follow the plan I laid out for you—then you, your family, and the animals will remain safe. Not only that, but on the 430th day aboard your ark, I will be there to greet you as you take your first step ashore.

"Oh, and by the way, I need to mention that you have 120 years to accomplish this task!" the Visitor exclaimed.

Without another word, the Visitor offered a wink, turned, and was gone as quickly as he had come.

Perplexed by what had just happened, each Noah naturally did what any confused (and wise) man would do. He sought the council of his wife.

At home, each Noah shared the story offered to him by the mysterious stranger with his wife. He told the tale exactly as it had been communicated to him by the Visitor.

It was at that definitive moment, when each Noah finished telling the story to his wife, that each would embark on his own unique journey. And though that journey might have begun in exactly the same fashion, it would take four strikingly different paths, determined by each Noah's unique choice and plan of action!

From this point forward, in an effort to help you identify with each Noah and understand each man's unique journey, I will refer to them as:

Noah the Thinker, Noah the Doer, Noah the Quitter and Noah the Great

Noah the Thinker

Noah the Great

Noah the Quitter

Noah the Doer

AND THEN THERE WERE FOUR

I SUPPOSE IT IS RATHER IRONIC. Each of the four Noahs began the race from the same starting point, were given the exact same information, under what amounted to the same conditions.

Yet the Noahs weren't competing against one another. None of the four Noahs knew anything about the other three, nor had they even considered the possibility of anyone else being faced with the Visitor's tasks. In fact, it wasn't much of a race at all, except against time.

Although each of the Noahs was given the same starting point, it didn't take long to see that their journeys—and thus the outcomes—would be vastly different.

NOAH THE THINKER

FOLLOWING THE VISIT from the wise and mysterious Visitor, Noah the Thinker did what he most enjoyed: *he thought*. He thought about everything the Visitor had said about the Great Flood, building an ark, savings pairs of animals, and most importantly, saving his family.

Noah the Thinker thought about it, and thought about it, and thought about it. As he thought, he said to himself, "I have no reason whatsoever to doubt the wise Visitor. He seemed very knowledgeable and trustworthy."

Noah the Thinker continued to think. He thought about what he had been asked to do—specifically, to build a giant ark.

As Noah thought about the giant ark, he thought to himself the most obvious thought, "I am no carpenter. Sure, I have hammered a nail here and there, but build a 450-foot boat?"

Despite his limited background in carpentry, Noah the Thinker remained confident. "I can do it. I will build an amazing ark!"

With each passing day, Noah the Thinker thought about it, and thought about it, and thought about it. In fact, he couldn't get it out of his mind. He delighted in the notion that he had been called upon to carry out this task by the stranger, and that he had been deemed "special."

Every once in a while, Noah the Thinker would think to himself, "If I am going to build a giant ark, and spend over a year on board with thousands of animals, I should probably learn how to build things," and he would pick up a book on woodworking.

When Noah the Thinker wasn't reading books on woodworking, he was reading books about animals. "If I am going to be aboard an ark with thousands of animals for over a year, I should probably know a thing or two about animals."

With each passing day, Noah the Thinker's level of confidence grew. He felt inspired, and he felt like he was training his mind for great things.

"No wonder the stranger picked me," thought Noah the Thinker. "Look at all I have done to learn about woodworking and about animals."

Twenty years passed. Noah the Thinker had read hundreds of books on the topics of woodworking and animals. He was proud of all he had learned and felt more confident than ever that he was up to the task.

As a result of Noah the Thinker's confidence and his hard work over the past two decades, Noah the Thinker determined it was time for a well-deserved vacation.

Throughout the next ten years, Noah the Thinker took some time to enjoy himself.

One day, Noah the Thinker's wife said to him, "Noah, dear. Thirty years have gone by since the wise stranger visited you. Don't you think that it is about time you start building the ark?"

Noah the Thinker looked up at her and smiled, "Nonsense, dear! The Visitor said the flood wouldn't come for 120 years. I have plenty of time."

Noah the Thinker's wife looked quizzically at her husband. She had her doubts. Building the ark was quite a large project, but she trusted her husband. With that, she smiled a rather hesitant smile, and walked away.

Despite his confident reply, Noah the Thinker did believe it was time to refocus. After taking ten years off to relax, he felt refreshed. It was now time to turn his attention back to the ark.

Noah the Thinker had another thought. "All I know is that I am supposed to build an ark that is 450 feet long, 50 feet wide, and 30 feet tall."

With that, Noah the Thinker took out his pen and a sketchpad. He also went to his bookshelf and grabbed an armful of books on various topics of design.

Excitement raced through Noah the Thinker's brain and he conjured up countless thoughts and ideas. "This is going to be the best and coolest-looking ark ever!" he thought to himself.

With each passing day, Noah the Thinker was consumed by the glorious thoughts of what his ark might look like.

He considered everything from aerodynamics to aesthetics. He thought about magnificent built-in features he affectionately called "creature com-forts" on each on of his sketches.

As the years went by, Noah the Thinker drafted thousands upon thousands of sketches, and wrote down even more ideas that were never included in any particular sketch.

After years of compiling notes and drafting glorious sketches, Noah the Thinker looked up from his sketchpad. Standing at the door was his lovely wife.

"Noah, dear," she began. "You have been at this project for quite some time. You have read hundreds, if not thousands, of books. You have created even more designs—so many, in fact, that they are piled to the ceiling, filling our closets, the space under our beds, and in our cupboards. We can scarcely move around the house anymore because of all of your drawings."

As Noah the Thinker looked around the house, he could see that she was entirely correct. He thought to himself, "We are up to our necks in paper. It is like we are drowning in it."

Noah the Thinker continued to survey his surroundings. With his hand stroking his white beard, he thought about it, and thought about it, and thought about it. After giving it some serious consideration, he walked up to one of three easels in the corner of the room.

"This is it!" he exclaimed. "This is the ark that I am going to build for us!" he said with excitement.

Standing in the doorway, Noah the Thinker's wife once again smiled a rather hesitant smile, and walked away.

Although eighty years had since passed from the time Noah the Thinker was visited by the wise stranger, Noah the Thinker was still confident that he would get the job done.

He had studied hard for twenty years, learning all he needed to know about woodworking, architecture, and design.

He had invested fifty years in meticulously designing the perfect ship.

He was now ready!

Noah the Thinker then realized that before building the ark, he would need to gather his supplies.

Noah the Thinker grabbed his trusty saw and made his way out back. He looked up at the tall trees.

"Which of you is ready to become an ark?" he asked with a smile.

With that, Noah the Thinker made his way into the woods and began cutting down the trees.

110 Years Later

WITH ONLY TEN YEARS TO GO, Noah the Thinker came to realize that building the ark was more work than he anticipated. While he had given himself forty years to build his ark, he realized that he was only about a third of the way finished, with only ten years to go.

Noah the Thinker thought about giving up, but quickly dismissed the thought from his mind.

"I can do this!" he exclaimed confidently.

With the majority of the project still ahead of him, Noah the Thinker devised a new plan. Rather than working eight hours each day, he would now work twelve hours per day. Rather than working six days per week, he would now work seven. Clear the tracks! It was full steam ahead for Noah the Thinker.

NOAH THE DOER

FOLLOWING THE VISIT from the wise and mysterious stranger, whom he began to think of as "the Visitor," Noah the Doer did what he most often did: *he did.*

He grabbed his trusty saw and immediately made his way toward the woods to begin cutting down trees. Noah the Doer cut, and cut, and cut. He cut for days—and then weeks—and then months—and then years.

Noah the Doer continued to cut until he had cut down just about every tree in sight.

As Noah looked around, he could not help but be impressed, "Look at all my lumber!" he exclaimed. "Imagine the great and glorious things I could build with all of this wood!"

In what seemed like no time at all, Noah the Doer had enough wood to build his ark. In fact, it was more likely that Noah the Doer had cut down enough wood to build ten arks!

With gusto and without haste, Noah the Doer put down his saw, picked up his hammer, grabbed his nails, and began the construction of his ark.

Noah the Doer hammered away. Both his great skill and strong work ethic allowed him to construct the frame of the ark in what seemed like no time, once again.

As Noah the Doer took a step back to admire his work up to this point, he paused a moment to look around. He quickly realized that he had harvested more wood than he would ever need to build his ark.

He waved his hammer back and forth. He had been so caught up in doing that he had failed to think much about what the mysterious Visitor had said to him.

When Noah the Doer did stop doing for a moment and consider the stranger's words, what he chose to recall was quite selective.

"The Visitor came to me because I am special. He knows that I can build anything, so he asked me to build an ark," Noah the Doer thought to himself.

"You know what?" Noah the Doer said. "I will do the Visitor one better. Look at all the wood I harvested. Instead of building a small ship, I will build a massive fortress. I will build it to the clouds so that not even all of the water on Earth could reach the top.

With each passing day, Noah the Doer's structure grew. He felt accomplished, and he felt like his building would far surpass the expectations of the stranger and the ark.

"It's no wonder the Visitor picked me," thought Noah the Doer. "Just look at what I have built."

After sixty years, Noah the Doer was just ahead of his halfway point. Noah the Doer was proud of his massive structure. It was already the tallest building on Earth, and he was confident that even if the flood came today, he and his family would be safe.

Nonetheless, Noah the Doer pressed forward. He was determined to use all the wood available to him, and was committed to erecting a building for all ages.

It was around this time that Noah the Doer's wife asked, "Noah, dear, don't you think you should follow directions and build the ark like you were instructed?"

Noah the Doer replied, "Nonsense, dear! Who needs a simple boat when I can create a building that will reach the heavens?"

Noah the Doer's wife had her doubts. Surely there was a reason the Visitor had instructed the construction of such an ark, but she trusted her husband. With that, she smiled a rather hesitant smile, and walked away.

Noah the Doer built. . .and built. . .and built. He worked tirelessly, and his effort was surely unequal to that of anyone else.

"This is going to be the best and largest edifice ever!" he thought to himself.

Noah the Doer paused for a moment. "Look at all I have done. My building is massive." Stroking his white beard with his work-callused hand, it quickly dawned on him. "It needs more!"

"Detail!" he exclaimed. "It needs detail—but not just any detail. It needs the finest detail." He cheered with excitement.

Standing in the doorway, Noah the Doer's wife once again smiled a rather hesitant smile, and turned away.

With his magnificent tower reaching the heavens after only ninety years of work, Noah the Doer was now proudly working on etching one-of-a-kind works of art into the wood throughout his structure.

His etchings included stories, and symbols, and even areas to play games. There was no detail too small or any detail that would be overlooked.

"If I am going to spend over a year within the walls of this building, along with my family, such details will be important, " he thought to himself.

With that, Noah the Doer made his way through his enormous building, etching story after story, symbol after symbol, and game after game, into the walls of his wooden fortress.

110 Years Later

WITH TEN YEARS TO GO, Noah the Doer had constructed not only the largest building on the face of the Earth, he had also managed to make it the most majestic.

His woodwork and craftsmanship were glorious. His detailed artwork scattered throughout the structure was unrivaled. People came from miles away to marvel at his work.

"Wait until the Visitor returns," Noah the Doer said to himself. "He wanted me to build a tiny and insignificant ship. Just wait until he sees what I have constructed!"

NOAH THE QUITTER

FOLLOWING THE VISIT from the wise and mysterious Visitor, Noah the Quitter appeared to care little about what had been asked of him.

Sure, he had heard the voice, and it was true that he understood every word the Visitor had uttered.

However, Noah the Quitter was not interested. He was not interested in the Great Flood, he was not interested in the animals, and he was certainly not interested in building a massive ark!

"Such a project was far too much work, and who was this Visitor anyway? What if the guy was some crazy old fool who had no idea what he was talking about?" thought Noah the Quitter.

"In fact, that's it! I am sure of it," he said to himself. "He was just some crazy person telling me to do something he knows I cannot do. That way, he can watch and laugh at me from a distance while I try and build his stupid boat."

Noah the Quitter mocked the Visitor. "Who does he think he is? I am no one special. He knows it—and I know it. Build a 450-foot ark? I have never picked up a tool in my life. Save animals? I don't know the first thing about animals," he muttered spitefully.

As he thought about it more and more, the angrier Noah the Quitter got.

Noah the Quitter looked around. He looked far into the distance; he looked up into the mountains; he looked into the trees; he looked everywhere. He was sure the mysterious Visitor was watching him and waiting for him to try to build the giant ark, so the Visitor could laugh at him.

"I'm not falling for it. I am simply not," he repeated to himself over and over.

"The flood isn't my problem. There are other people out there who are supposed to deal with problems like that. Why doesn't the old fool go talk to a carpenter so he can build it, or some rich financers, so they can commission a project?" he exclaimed.

"The government! That's it!" Noah the Quitter shouted. "This is the government's problem. The government is supposed to help people, and if this flood is as massive as the Visitor said it's going to be, then it's the government's responsibility to figure out a way to save everyone!"

Noah the Quitter lay in his hammock, enjoying the sun. He couldn't help but laugh at everyone else around him. Look at all of the worker bees, scurrying off to work. "What a miserable and thankless life," he thought to himself.

After fifty years, Noah the Quitter reflected on the long-ago visit from the stranger. Although he was sure he didn't want to put in the time to work on an ark, and that he was incapable of building such a boat even if he wanted to, he couldn't help but feel anxious.

Nonetheless, Noah the Quitter continued to do what he had always done. He quit. He quit on the Visitor. He quit on the animals. He quit on his family. And of course, he quit on himself.

It was around this time that Noah the Quitter's wife said to him, "Noah, dear, what if the Visitor WAS correct? What if there is a flood?"

Noah the Quitter replied, "You worry too much. Plus, I can't build an ark. I don't know the first thing about building things. You know that."

Listening to her husband, she acknowledged his limited skills, but nevertheless challenged him,

"You did say that the Visitor told you that you had 120 years to build the ark. Maybe you could study for a few years, practice your craft, and then work on building the ark? You still have seventy years."

To which Noah the Quitter replied, "That is A LOT of work, dear! If you believe some great flood is coming, why don't you work on building the ark yourself?"

Looking at the ground, she attempted to smile. She managed to give a rather half-hearted smile as she slowly walked away.

Noah the Quitter watched his wife. "The nerve of that woman! Asking me to study, to practice, and then to build a giant ark, all for something that may—or may not—ever happen."

As he stared, he stewed. And as he stewed, he stared.

Why was this supposed flood his problem anyway? Why was he expected to build a giant boat? He continued his rant. "With all the craftsmen and worker bees out there, couldn't the Visitor go harass one of them?"

With that, Noah the Quitter sank into a state of resentment. "This isn't my problem, and I see no reason why I should have to be the one to fix it!"

110 Years Later

WITH TEN YEARS TO GO, Noah the Quitter cared little. Sure, he was anxious. Sure, he was full of doubt, living day to day with great uncertainty, but as far as the actual ark was concerned, he had no more interest in it today than he had 110 years before.

"Even if there is a flood, which I sincerely doubt there will be, someone will come to my rescue. The stranger probably found some sucker to build a big boat...maybe even my wife."

As Noah the Quitter looked around, he wondered if his wife had ever started on building her own boat. "I mean, she did have the audacity to expect me to do it. Obviously she thought it was important. I wonder if she decided to build one?" he thought to himself.

NOAH THE GREAT

FOLLOWING THE VISIT from the wise and mysterious Visitor, Noah the Great did what he often did—*he planned.*

He thought about everything the Visitor had said about the Great Flood: building an ark, saving the animals in pairs, and most importantly, saving his family.

After giving his situation some thought, Noah the Great quickly realized, "I need to learn how to build an ark."

Despite his limited background in carpentry, Noah the Great remained confident, "I can do it. I will build an amazing ark!"

Noah the Great quickly began to gather as much information as he could about woodworking, carpentry, and architecture.

While the Visitor had told Noah the Great that he needed to build an ark that was 450 feet long, 50 feet wide, and 30 feet high, the Visitor had not told Noah the Great *HOW* to build such boat, he realized.

Noah the Great understood that learning how to build the ark was up to him, and that he would need to study hard in order to build it well.

As Noah the Great studied, he also practiced. He built small-scale models and tested them on the open waters to make sure his designs were structurally sound.

The more he learned, the more he applied his craft, and the more he applied his craft, the better his models became.

After twenty years of studying and building scale models, Noah the Great believed that he was ready to begin working on his ark.

He worked diligently each day, from 8 o'clock in the morning until 5 o'clock in the evening, six days each week, only to rest on the seventh.

At night, he spent time with his wife and children, tending to his husbandly and fatherly duties. Noah the Great always felt that having a balance among the many priorities of his life actually helped him accomplish more and to be more successful at each endeavor.

As with anything in life, Noah the Great encountered setbacks. There were some times the wood pieces he cut did not fit quite right. There were other times his tools broke. There were even times the weather itself failed to cooperate, being too hot, too cold, or too rainy, to work.

Yet, despite these obstacles, Noah the Great continued to make progress.

He built and studied, built and studied—realizing that if he wanted to create a quality product, a key to his success would be consistent and honest effort.

As Noah the Great worked and studied, his wife remained by his side, offering encouragement throughout the process.

"Noah, dear, I am very proud of you. You work tirelessly each day, paying close attention to detail, so when the day of the Great Flood comes, our family will be saved," she said to him.

Understanding that the Visitor's words had carried with them both a gift and a responsibility, Noah the Great took joy in his work each day, for he realized that one day, he would be able to harvest the fruits of his labors.

110 Years Later

WITH TEN YEARS TO GO, Noah the Great worked neither harder nor slower than he had in days past. Because of his careful planning and consistent effort, he remained on schedule.

He continued to work eight hours each day, six days a week, as he had each day of the previous 110 years. He continued to devote the appropriate amount of time to his wife and children, who at the time were already in the process of helping him collect pairs of each animal to bring aboard the ark.

With most of the ark now complete, and most of the animals collected and aboard, Noah the Great and his family remained confident that when the Great Flood did in fact come, they would be ready for it.

BATTEN DOWN THE HATCHES

As the wise Visitor had promised, 120 years from the time of his visit, a storm began brewing.

Each of the four Noahs, although thousands of miles apart, were experiencing the same fateful storm the Visitor had promised would occur so many years before.

The clouds blackened, the winds howled, and the trees begin to rock from side to side. Noah the Thinker, Noah the Doer, Noah the Quitter, and Noah the Great each began to reflect on the last 120 years.

* * * * *

Noah the Thinker thought to himself, "Why did the Visitor pick me? If he was so wise, surely he would have known that I would fail. Look at my ark. It is nowhere near complete. There was simply not enough time to build such a ship, and I am sure the stranger knew it."

Noah the Thinker continued to think back about the last 120 years. He had spent not just years, but decades, learning about how to construct an ark.

Not only did he study, but he planned. For fifty years, he had worked on designing the perfect ark, making certain not to forget a single detail of what he learned while studying.

Noah the Thinker compiled sketch after sketch, took note after note, until he was certain that the design he selected was the right one.

As Noah the Thinker thought more and more about his situation, the more frustrated he got, not even stopping a moment to consider the ten years he had taken off in between.

"It took me eighty years to learn how to build and design your ark, and you expected that somehow I would be able to build it in but forty? Curse you, old man! Curse you!" he shouted off into the distance.

Noah the Thinker felt betrayed. What good was having this knowledge of the Great Flood if there was no way to save himself or his family?

Noah the Thinker and his half-finished ark

* * * * *

Noah the Doer thought to himself, "No wonder the Visitor picked me. Just look at my building. No man on Earth has ever created anything like it!"

Noah the Doer continued to think back about the last 120 years. He had spent not just years, but decades, toiling away. He had worked, and worked, and worked.

He had worked, and he had worked hard. It was back-breaking labor to saw as many logs as he did, haul them into place, and build a building from the Earth's surface to Heaven's gates.

Not only did Noah the Doer perform such back-breaking labor, but he also demonstrated exquisite detail. His artwork and carvings were crafted with great care.

As Noah the Doer thought more and more about his situation, the more confident he grew.

"Over the past 120 years, no man on Earth has worked as hard as I have. It is no wonder the wise Visitor picked me. I deserve to be saved, along with my family," Noah the Doer said with great pride.

Noah the Doer and his magnificent tower

* * * * *

Noah the Quitter thought to himself, "Who cares? Even if this storm is as bad as the crazy man said it would be, who cares?"

Noah the Quitter continued to reflect on the last 120 years. "While the rest of these suckers have toiled away, day after day, at their menial jobs, I have enjoyed life."

Noah the Quitter was correct in but one of two respects. While everyone around him had been working hard and he managed to get by doing very little at all, it turned out that he did not exactly enjoy life.

As Noah the Quitter thought more and more about his situation, to say he "enjoyed life" was not necessarily true. Although he did very little, he was getting more anxious with each passing day.

In addition to being anxious, he began to get the sense that he had wasted his life—not to mention the opportunity afforded to him by the Visitor to save himself and his family.

Noah the Quitter got depressed. "If I would have known what I know today, maybe I would have given that boat a try," he said regretfully.

As Noah the Quitter usually did in such situations, he flopped into his hammock and felt sorry for himself.

Noah the Quitter without an ark

* * * * *

Noah the Great thought to himself, "It appears the time has come." Looking at the blackened sky, he called for his wife and his children to make their way to the ark.

Noah the Great reflected on the last 120 years. He could not help but feel humbled and was overwhelmed by a deep sense of appreciation for the visit paid to him by the wise Visitor.

"Of the thousands of people on Earth, he came to me, a man with very few skills and of equally modest means. He could have picked a king, or a nobleman, or a wise scholar, but he picked me," thought Noah.

As Noah the Great's family joined him, he put his arms around them. He smiled at his wife and she kissed him softly on the lips and thanked him.

Confused, Noah the Great asked her, "And what is it exactly that you are thanking me for?" he asked sincerely. "Had it not been for the gift of wisdom offered by the Visitor, surely we would all be doomed. You should be thanking him, not me," Noah the Great said to his wife.

His wife looked deep into his eyes and replied, "True, we do owe our deepest gratitude to the wise Visitor, but you did this, Noah. It was you who listened to the Visitor, toiled day after day after day, to build this magnificent ark. For 120 years, eight hours each day, six days each week, you gave your best. It is for this, Noah, that I thank you," she said to him.

Noah the Great and his ark

* * * * *

Suddenly, the winds picked up in intensity. Dark clouds stretched across the sky as far as the eye could see.

As the rain cascaded down, each Noah uttered the same words, almost in unison, across the great distances, "This is it."

* * * * *

When the waters rose, the first to be swept away was Noah the Quitter. He floated off into the distance and did not see any boats or anyone coming to his rescue.

At a time when he needed others the most, he finally realized the mistake he had made.

"Perhaps I should have listened to the stranger. He afforded me the opportunity to save myself, and my family, and I wasted it," he said as he paddled.

With barely enough time to even finish his thought, Noah the Quitter disappeared beneath the waves.

* * * * *

For days, it rained and rained and rained. The winds were relentless, showing no sign of mercy. Clinging to his partially completed ark, along with his family, Noah the Thinker tried to remain confident that they might be able to ride out the storm.

Despite his optimism, his family knew the truth. Without a completed boat, it would only be a matter of time before the storm got the better of them.

It was at that moment Noah the Thinker thought to himself, "How can this be happening? I had a plan. I had a wonderful plan. There just wasn't enough time. If only I had had more time," he lamented.

Although Noah the Thinker and his family tried to ride out the storm, it was simply too much and they also disappeared beneath the roiling waters.

* * * * *

For weeks, the rain came, and it continued to come hard. The Earth was now covered with water, without a speck of dry land in sight.

However, rising above the tremendous swell were Noah the Doer and his family in their majestic tower.

Although the waters were rising, Noah the Doer remained confident that not even all the water on Earth could reach the top of his building.

However, with each passing day, the currents picked up. Faster and faster, they swirled and eddied around his tower, as did the blustering wind.

The faster the currents got, the less confident Noah the Doer became. After several months, Noah the Doer and his family began to feel the foundation of the building begin to give way.

Sadly, Noah the Doer now realized that with months of wind, waves, and currents still ahead of them, it was only a matter of time before his building was swept away.

It was at that moment Noah the Doer thought to himself, "I worked hard. I worked so very hard. No man on Earth has worked as hard as I had."

"If only I had listened to the wise stranger. If only I had built the ark as he instructed me to do. It would have actually been less work, and clearly, been better for me and my family."

Sure enough, at his moment of realization, his glorious building gave way and was carried off by the swirling current.

* * * * *

For forty days and nights, it rained and rained and rained. The more it rained, the higher the water rose.

Despite the intense rain, Noah the Great and his family rode out the storm. Aboard the ark, they managed to enjoy the time they had together, unshaken by the treacherous conditions surrounding them.

Noah the Great reflected about the visit from the wise Visitor. Notwithstanding his good fortune, Noah didn't feel "special," as the Visitor had called him. In fact, he felt no more special now then he had moments before meeting the Visitor.

As he continued to reflect, Noah the Great also remembered the Visitor had instructed him not to cut corners.

Noah the Great looked at his ark, content with what he had built. He had taken time early on in the process to study woodworking and carpentry. He also tested what he learned by building small-scale models.

Lastly, Noah the Great made sure to follow the precise instructions he had been given: 450 feet long, 50 feet wide, and 30 feet tall.

With each passing day for 120 years, Noah the Great had gone about his work. He had cared little about the work or accomplishments of those around him.

Noah the Great had not been focused on what others had or were doing, for he recognized his fulfillment would never come from comparing himself and his actions. Rather, his fulfillment was based on doing his best in all aspects of his life.

Sure, on occasion, he remembered looking around to see what others were up to, but never did it sway him off course or lead him to question his own work.

Noah the Great also understood his own mission and his own purpose. His purpose was to build an ark—and build an ark he did.

On the 430th day, the waters had receded and land emerged all around. Noah the Great greeted the sunrise with a smile. He knew this was the day—the day that he would finally be able to disembark onto dry land.

As the sun made its way over the horizon, Noah the Great noticed a man approaching from a great distance.

It appeared that someone else had also managed to remain safe during the Great Flood.

As the man neared, Noah the Great realized that it was, in fact, the Visitor.

"Greetings, my boy!" shouted the Visitor.

Noah looked at him and smiled.

"Did you not remember my promise to you to come greet you on the 430th day when you once again walked upon the shore?" asked the Visitor.

"Now I do," Noah said, smiling matter-of- factly.

The Visitor turned to Noah's family, greeting each member with open arms. Noah the Great's wife looked at the Visitor and said, "Thank you."

The Visitor replied with a smile. "Don't thank me. Thank Noah. It was Noah who took the time to learn how to build this ark. It was Noah who

practiced his skills, making sure not to cut any corners. Noah believed in himself, had a plan, and worked in earnest with each passing day."

Noah the Great understood what the Visitor was saying, but he still couldn't help but wonder, "Why me?"

Noah the Great looked at the Visitor and said, "I am no one special. There were thousands of others you could have gone to, and thousands of others who were not afforded the same fate as my family and me. So I ask you, why did you choose me?"

The Visitor raised his hand, put it on Noah's shoulder, and said to him, "Everyone is special, born with special talents and abilities. I went to others, telling them exactly what I told you. However, you were the only one who listened. You were the only one who embraced how special you are, worked hard each day, and thus realized your potential."

SUCCESS IS UP TO YOU

IT IS MY HOPE that as you read through this book, you recognize and understand that we are all Noah, and that we may be different Noahs at different times.

Sometimes, we may get stuck on developing a plan, believe that we have so many great ideas, but fail to act on them—like Noah the Thinker.

There are times we may feel like we are the hardest working person at our company or in our field, but are we really being productive or merely being active—like Noah the Doer?

There are times we may feel like quitting or that we are simply not up to the task. There may be times that we accept our shortcomings and allow ourselves to be content with relying on others rather than relying on ourselves—like Noah the Quitter.

Sometimes, however, every once in a while, we realize our potential. We are faced with a difficult situation or task, and we rise to the challenge. We develop a plan, work hard, give our best, and accomplish our goals—like Noah the Great.

Each of us is very special. Each of us possesses amazing potential to accomplish great things. Oftentimes, however, we get in our own way. As a result, we fail to realize our true potential.

Take Noah the Thinker, for example. Noah the Thinker studied, and planned, and planned. He wanted to succeed, and he knew that he had it in himself to do so.

However, as much as Noah the Thinker had in desire, he lacked in execution. He put off actually DOING the work for so long that by the time he did start his work, there simply was not enough time for him to complete the project.

Now consider Noah the Doer. Noah the Doer worked hard. He worked, and worked, and worked. It was impossible to deny that Noah the Doer was among the hardest working people of his day.

However, as hard as Noah the Doer worked, he failed when it came to productivity. He was given a very specific set of directions, which he failed to deliver upon. Instead he opted to do it HIS WAY, which he eventually learned was a mistake.

Now let's consider Noah the Quitter. Noah the Quitter did not believe in himself, nor did he believe those who tried to help him. He refused to accept any responsibility for his own well-being and assumed that in a moment of great need, SOMEONE ELSE would be there to bail him out.

Lastly, we have Noah the Great ...

Noah the Great listened. He appreciated those who tried to help him. When provided with guidelines, he was humble enough to accept them. He then took it upon himself to educate himself and develop the best plan to execute against the guidelines.

He always put in an honest day's work, without anyone forcing him to do so. He gave his best effort without any inclination to cut corners. With a deep sense of purpose, he learned to take joy in his work.

* * * * *

In the end, each Noah reaped the appropriate fruits of his labors (or lack thereof).

Noah the Quitter was quickly swept away by the flood waters.

Noah the Thinker lasted a little longer, but his ideas and planning could only take him so far.

Noah the Doer, by virtue of his hard work, fared well for some time, but eventually succumbed to the same fate as the others because of his stubbornness and because he had to do things his own way.

Noah the Great worked harder than Noah the Quitter, but not as hard as Noah the Doer. He planned more than the Noah the Doer, but not as long or as much as Noah the Thinker.

For Noah the Great to achieve his goal, he didn't have to be the best at any one thing ... he just had to be good at several different things, have proper balance in his life, and give an honest effort.

Noah the Great gave his best and stayed the course, each day focusing on his goal, which is why he was GREAT!

LESSONS FROM THE FOUR NOAHS

What key lesson can we learn from Noah the Thinker?

It is great to create a plan, but only if the plan is developed well and then is executed. Eventually, we need to put the great ideas on paper and begin constructing. If we wait too long, we will run out of time to complete our project.

DO NOT PUT OFF UNTIL TOMORROW
WHAT YOU CAN ACCOMPLISH TODAY.

What key lesson can we learn from Noah the Doer?

It is great to work hard, but hard work will only pay off when we focus our time and effort in the right areas. It is vitally important to recognize and understand that there is a difference between activity and productivity. It is not simply enough to be active and hard-working.

In addition, what Noah the Doer failed to see was that this task was not about him—he lost sight of what was important and did not prioritize.

It is far better to be productive, and spend our time and effort working on the right tasks.

MANAGE YOUR TIME AND EFFORTS WISELY BY FOCUSING ON ACTIVITIES THAT WILL ALLOW YOU TO ACHIEVE YOUR PURPOSE AND REACH YOUR GOALS.

What key lesson can we learn from Noah the Quitter?

When times get tough, we need to take responsibility for ourselves. The only person we can truly rely on or have any control over is ourself. We cannot look to others, or expect that others will solve our problems for us.

While it may be easier to wait and hope for others to solve our problems for us, hope is not a solution. There will always be some people, no matter how much support or time they are given, who will continue to look toward others to bail them out.

WE ARE THE MASTERS OF OUR OWN DESTINY.
IN THE LONG RUN, WE WILL GET WHAT WE
TRULY DESERVE.

What key lesson can we learn from Noah the Great?

No matter how big the challenge, or how impossible something may seem, we can achieve great things.

It is all right to have ARK-sized goals. While a particular goal may seem impossible to others, if you develop a good plan, work hard each day, give your best effort, and understand that achieving great things takes time, you are capable of accomplishing your goals and realizing your dream.

WE ARE CAPABLE OF ACHIEVING GREAT THINGS
IF WE ARE WILLING TO GIVE IT OUR BEST SHOT.

Like most biblical stories, there are lessons to be learned. In considering the story of Noah and his ark, I can see parallels in my own life—as I am sure you can as well.

I believe that I have a responsibility as a husband and father to care for the needs, and in many cases, the wants, of my family, to provide them with shelter, and to protect them from dangers in life. I believe that I possess abilities, both physical and mental, that serve as tools to accomplish these goals.

In addition to those beliefs, I am also certain it is necessary to put in a considerable amount of effort. It is my responsibility and choice to get up out of bed each morning with a purpose, and use my tools to continue to build a quality environment for my family, as well as others.

I also realize that not everyone views or approaches life in the same way. Across society, and particularly in adults, people exhibit a broad range of beliefs they have in themselves and in the effort they put forth in their daily pursuits. I have divided these variances into four quadrants:

High Belief	High Belief
Low Effort	High Effort
Noah the Thinker	*Noah the Great*
Low Belief	Low Belief
Low Effort	High Effort
Noah the Quitter	*Noah the Doer*

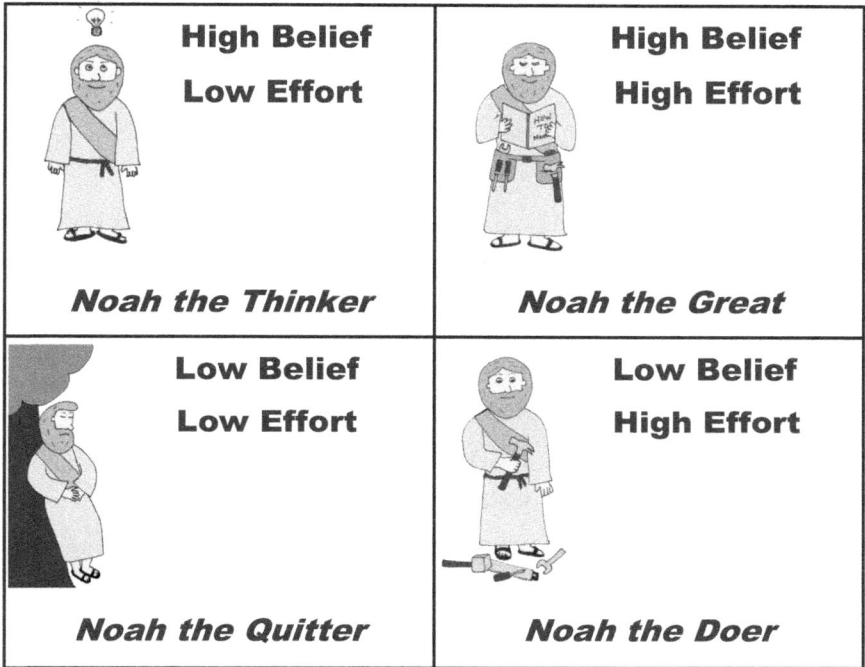

It was from this simple diagram that I was able to successfully build out the narrative of *Four Noahs*.

It is my sincere hope that you enjoyed this book, and as a result of reading it, you are able to apply lessons in your own life to accomplish your goals and realize your dreams.

SUCCESS IS NO ACCIDENT

**IT IS HARD WORK,
PERSEVERANCE,
LEARNING,
STUDYING,
SACRIFICE, AND MOST OF ALL,
LOVE OF WHAT YOU ARE DOING.**

- PELE -

AFTERWORD

BETWEEN 2014 AND 2015, I BEGAN developing and mapping out the framework for this book. However, *Four Noahs* did not truly become clear for me until February 22, 2015—the day everything finally clicked!

My wife, daughter Kensington, and I were attending mass at our parish. It was the beginning of the Lenten season and the homily made reference to Noah and his ark. This book project had been on my mind quite a bit during that time, and whether by divine intervention or simply coincidence, I experienced a moment of clarity.

The reason Noah the Great experienced success was because his belief was strong AND he put forth considerable effort. Genesis 6:1 says that God sought out Noah for a noble purpose. Equally important, if perhaps not more so, Noah the Great listened to God and honored His wishes.

It was also in Genesis that we learned that building the ark was no easy task. According to the Bible, Noah's ark was approximately 450 feet long, 45 feet wide, and was divided into three levels. While it is unclear exactly how long it took Noah to build such a vessel, many

Christians accept the belief that it took Noah at least 55 years, to as many as 120 years, from beginning to end.

In the case of Noah the Great, we learn about a man who was a believer. He believed that he had a purpose and also believed he was capable of achieving it.

In addition to his strong belief, he also put in an incredible amount of effort and time. As a result of Noah the Great's strong belief in himself, and his effort, he was able to save his family, many of God's creatures, and himself.

ABOUT THE AUTHOR

Brian A. Peters is an award-winning author and professor at the Milwaukee School of Engineering in the Rader School of Business. As an author, speaker, and consultant, his work centers on improvement, systems, and outcomes. He received his B.A. at the University of Wisconsin–Whitewater, where he studied psychology; received his M.B.A. at the University of Colorado at Colorado Springs; his M.S.A. at Central Michigan University; and earned his M.Ed. at California Coast University, with an emphasis on Curriculum and Instruction.

He currently lives in Wisconsin with his wife, Missy, his daughters, Kensington and McKinley, along with their family dog, Sadie.

www.ingramcontent.com/pod-product-compliance
Lightning Source LLC
Chambersburg PA
CBHW031218270326
41931CB00006B/605